PIANO SOLO

THE RISE OF SKYWALKER

ISBN 978-1-5400-8334-0

Visit Hal Leonard Online at
www.halleonard.com

Contact us:
Hal Leonard
7777 West Bluemound Road
Milwaukee, WI 53213
Email: info@halleonard.com

In Europe, contact:
Hal Leonard Europe Limited
42 Wigmore Street
Marylebone, London, W1U 2RN
Email: info@halleonardeurope.com

In Australia, contact:
Hal Leonard Australia Pty. Ltd.
4 Lentara Court
Cheltenham, Victoria, 3192 Australia
Email: info@halleonard.com.au

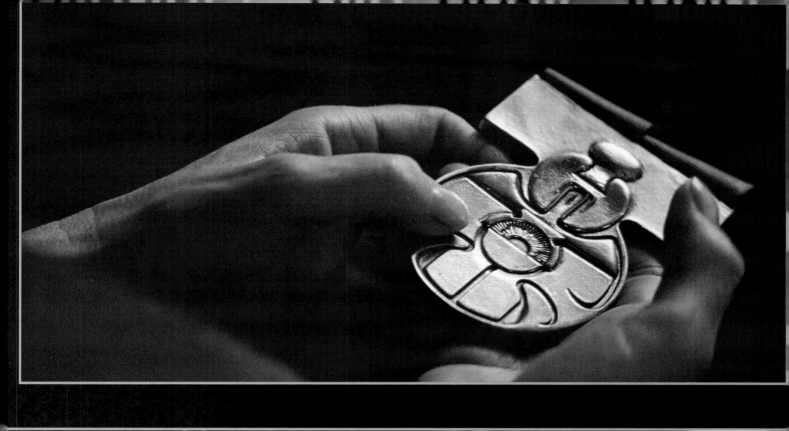

STAR WARS: THE RISE OF SKYWALKER

FANFARE *AND* PROLOGUE

Composed by
JOHN WILLIAMS

JOURNEY TO EXEGOL

Composed by
JOHN WILLIAMS

Moderately, forcefully

THE RISE OF SKYWALKER

Composed by
JOHN WILLIAMS

15

Slightly slower

rit.

Steadily, faster

mf

THE SPEEDER CHASE

Composed by
JOHN WILLIAMS

Moderately fast

DESTINY OF A JEDI

Composed by
JOHN WILLIAMS

Slowly, expressively

ANTHEM OF EVIL

Composed by
JOHN WILLIAMS

WE GO TOGETHER

Composed by
JOHN WILLIAMS

Moderately slow March

THE FINAL SABER DUEL

Composed by
JOHN WILLIAMS

BATTLE OF THE RESISTANCE

Composed by
JOHN WILLIAMS

Moderately fast relentlessly

FAREWELL

Composed by
JOHN WILLIAMS

REUNION

Composed by
JOHN WILLIAMS

A NEW HOME

Composed by
JOHN WILLIAMS

THE FORCE IS WITH YOU

Composed by
JOHN WILLIAMS